Trinity Training & Media

HOW TO CREATE A BASIC WEB SITE

Written by David Miller   B.S   M.S

Edited by Veronica Miller B.S   M.S

Trinity Technology and Media

524 Royal Greens Drive

Temple Terrace, FL 33617

Website: http://www.trinitytechnologymedia.com/

Facebook: http://www.facebook.com/trinitytechnologymedia

E-Mail: trinityt@trinitytechnologymedia.com

Alternate E-Mail: DMill8823@aol.com

About the Author

David Miller is an instructional designer in Tampa, Florida. He was educated at home by his mother, a certified teacher and experienced instructional designer. From kindergarten to high school, David was exposed to a technology-rich learning environment with a diverse curriculum. In addition to classroom instruction he had the opportunity to learn from using the computer, the Internet, CDs, field trips and self-directed projects. David took the SAT examination at fifteen and scored high enough to be accepted at most universities. But based on parental advice he enrolled at Hillsborough Community College to begin his undergraduate education. Upon graduation from the University of South Florida he received a Bachelor's Degree in Information Technology. After obtaining his first degree, David decided to pursue a master's degree in the field of education; specifically to design educational courses and programs. He selected Walden University and enrolled in the fall of 2011. In January 2014, David graduated with an impressive GPA and an MS in Instructional Design and Technology. To date he is involved with designing several courses for in class and online delivery, as well as authoring technical books.

Purpose of this Book

This book is written to teach anyone who is interested in developing a basic web site for business or personal use. Learners will have the opportunity to attain necessary HTML skills and knowledge to create their web site. The content is written with the non-technical user in mind. Yet it covers all that is required for creating multiple web pages and designing an effective web site using HTML. Beginning with a brief history of the Internet, users will be able to understand the context of its development, utility and technology. They will learn the rudiments of hypertext markup language (HTML) applicable for website development, and simple web design skills. Additionally, the book will introduce users to other related Internet resources such as social networks and some commonly used web design applications.

TABLE OF CONTENTS

About the Author..3

Purpose of this Book..4

INTRODUCING THE INTERNET AND HTML 7

WHAT IS THE INTERNET? 8

History...8

MAJOR ELEMENTS OF THE INTERNET 9

Intranets/Extranets..9

Ethernet..9

Routers 9

Servers 10

Browsers 10

E-Mail..10

Navigation 10

Internet Security...11

Computer Security 11

Cybersecurity..12

Examples of Security Programs 12

WHAT IS HTML?...13

Tags..13

Elements...13

Attributes..13

STARTING A WEB PAGE...16

HTML Editors 17

Opening Notepad..18

Selecting the Font..18

Elements...19

Adding Tags...20

Headings...23

Adding Text..24

Pictures...25

Saving the File 26

Changing the Font Size 27

Adding text to the Web Page 28

Check Your Progress 29

ADDING WEB PAGES **32**

Creating a Link 33

Links 33

Creating the New Page 34

Adding a Photo 35

Linking to a Page 36

Using Images as Links 42

Check Your Progress 44

OTHER HTML FEATURES **46**

Managing Fonts 47

Creating Backgrounds 48

Generating Lists 52

Inserting Tables 55

Check Your Progress 57

CREATING A BLOG **61**

What is a Blog? 62

Creating a Blog 62

References: 64

Publishing the Blog 65

Check Your Progress 66

PUBLISHING YOUR WEBSITE **70**

The Publishing Process 71

Choosing a Domain Name 71

Selecting a Hosting Company 72

Editing the Site 73

Maintaining your Website 76

APPENDIX 1 ....**77**

Template for a Personal Web Page in HTML 77

APPENDIX 2 ....**80**

References 80

Chapter 1

Introducing the Internet and HTML

What is the Internet?

History

The Internet was first established in 1969 by the Advanced Research Projects Agency Network (ARPANET). This was spearheaded by the US Department of Defense. Beginning in the 1970s, e-mail and other messaging systems were created and distributed among large companies as well as government organizations. These systems allowed individuals in each organization to send messages to each other. However, problems arose with general refusal to allow interconnection of computers between organizations. Over time, issues like these made it necessary to establish rules that would enable various users to communicate (whether in organizations or not) on the Internet and send messages. By 1987, ARPANET was heavily congested on its telephone lines; thus, a network run by the National Science Foundation (NSFNet) merged with two other networks (CSNet and BITNET) to form a major network that can handle the increasing online traffic. The result was a contract with corporations such as IBM and Sprint to operate the network's main backbone (connections and technology that support large amounts of data). IBM and Sprint were also among the first companies to help provide commercial Internet access.

The Internet or World Wide Web (WWW) possesses global broadcasting capability that serves as a medium for information dissemination, collaboration, and interaction among individuals and their computers regardless of geographic location. Simply called the Web, this innovative channel of communication, utilizes technology as a way to access, send and share information. It is a vast network of interconnected computers and networks that link millions of businesses, agencies, institutions, and individuals. Structurally, the Internet consists mainly of web pages which are really documents, images and audio files containing immense amounts of information. Web pages are connected to one another via connections called hyperlinks. Viewing and interacting with web pages are possible because of the technical capabilities of web browsers. These technological programs allow users to view text, images, videos, and other multimedia. Normally, a website contains one or more web pages that are grouped together under a common theme, for personal, commercial or social purposes. When a computer connects to the Internet, it becomes a web client.

Major Elements of the Internet

Listed below are brief descriptions of some of the network systems, services, programs and devices that support and impact operation of a website on the Internet.

Intranets/Extranets

An intranet is an information portal designed for the internal communications of various businesses. They include enterprises, governments, industries and financial institutions. Compared to the Internet, intranets can be tailored specifically to meet the exact needs of businesses and organizations. Users of intranets consist mainly of managers and directors, support staff, customer service, and other stakeholders. Extranets are portals designed for businesses to provide external users such as important clients, industry partners, and suppliers with limited access to certain files on computer systems.

Ethernet

Ethernet is the physical connection method of cabling networking technologies for local area (LAN) and larger networks to a computer. Simply put it is the cable that connects a computer or other device to a router or network. Ethernet is known as arguably the most popular and most effective network technology in the world. Furthermore, it is the most widely-installed local area network (LAN) technology. There are industry standards that govern Ethernet communication to technology devices. These standards include how communication is provided for connected devices as well how they are attached to a common medium such as a router that provides a path where electronic signals travel. An Ethernet LAN typically uses coaxial cable or special grades of twisted pair wires. In recent times, it is more commonly a twisted pair or fiber optic cabling. Most home computers are connected to the Internet using either coaxial cable or wireless adapters.

Routers

Routers are electronic devices that provide the mechanism for computers to communicate with other computers in a network, or to connect to an intranet or the Internet. The primary function of a router is to access the best path to receive data from one device and to transmit it to another. The internet service provider (ISP) assigns an Internet Protocol (IP) address (example of an IP address: 175 . 16 . 235 . 2) for each of the devices that are connected to the router.

Servers

Basically, servers are computers which serve information to other computers and receive from them also. On the Internet, web servers are structured in networks that contain software and files that are capable of connecting with other computers online. The software continuously runs on a computer and allows other computers to upload and download documents. Each file is private; only the users of that network can access those files. There are many online companies such as Dot5Hosting, Hostmonster, iPage, Web.com, HostGator, and GoDaddy.com to host websites. These companies usually charge monthly fees for their hosting services.

Browsers

A Web browser is a computer program used for accessing sites or information on a network (as the World Wide Web) and view web pages on the Internet. Web browsers are created by software run on the computer to connect to various operating system software programs across the Internet. The most commonly used web browsers include America Online, Internet Explorer, Google Chrome, Mozilla Firefox, and YouTube Browser. Users can navigate between each page through hyperlinks (detailed in Navigation section).

E-Mail

Short for electronic mail, e-mails are electronic messages containing files, images, and/or other attachments sent through a network (online) to a specific individual or group. Most Internet providers allow users to send and receive e-mail messages. There are e-mail programs such as Microsoft Outlook or Mozilla Thunderbird. The most common way that users send and receive e-mail is through free online e-mail services or web mail such as AOL mail, Hotmail, Google Mail (Gmail), and Yahoo Mail.

Navigation

Web navigation refers to the process of going through (or navigating) on a webpage, or on a network of multiple information resources online. The primary user interface used for navigation is the web browser. The constant goal is to have a web navigation interface that helps to maximize usability. Most web browsers have a navigation toolbar with buttons of frequently used web commands such as "back", "reload", "stop", "print", "Home", etc. In the middle of the toolbar is the location (also called address or URL) bar, which describes the text box for entering a web address in the browser. A Uniform Resource Locator (URL) is a uniquely formatted text that web browsers and other software uses to help identify network resources (web pages, documents, graphics, etc.) on the Internet. There are four parts for the addressing scheme in a URL:

- Transfer protocol (http://) - set of rules necessary for transporting the files, the most common type of Internet protocol is HTTP.
- Domain name – unique name for the address on the host computer.
- Pathname - Directory or folder where file is stored.
- Name of the file.

Here is the navigation bar for America Online

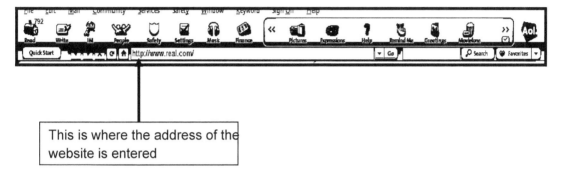

This is where the address of the website is entered

Internet Security

Internet security helps to establish rules and measures against attacks over the Internet. It involves not only browser security, but also network security in general as it relates to other applications and operating systems. Internet security programs monitor the exchange of information, and prevent intrusion or fraud. Different methods have been used to protect the transfer of data, including encryption, which refers to scrambling and encoding data transmission online, and preventing intruders from decoding and reading the page's content. The page is encrypted when there is a padlock icon at the bottom of the browser window. Web page security elements can be checked on the Internet Explorer.

Computer Security

Computer security is comprised of programs that are designed specifically for computing devices such as computers and smartphones used in both private and public settings such as the Internet. Functions of security applications involve protecting all the processes and mechanisms for digital equipment, information and services from viruses, malware and hacking. Computer security software detects and prevents unauthorized access or changes or destruction of information. It is becoming increasingly important to purchase this type of software to protect personal information and documents on PCs, smart phones, tablets and social media.

Cybersecurity

Cybersecurity is the overall process of utilizing security measures for data confidentiality, integrity, and availability. Cybersecurity protects assets such as the vast amounts of data on computers, servers, and cloud technology from hackers and unauthorized access. The goal of cybersecurity is to protect and ensure security of data. Some of the measures include access control, awareness training, risk assessment, security assessment, vulnerability management, etc. Cybersecurity functions are critical because web servers open windows between individual networks and the entire world virtually. Server maintenance, web application updates and website coding help to determine the degree of web security. Websites are prone to security risks, in addition to networks where web servers are connected. Furthermore, all programs either have bugs or weaknesses to varying degrees, since they are inherently complex . However, poorly written software exacerbates security issues, and the bugs will create web security issues that directly affect web applications and the server. In recent times, there have been cyber attacks against major corporations such as Target, Home Depot, Neiman Marcus and Sony. The combination of technical factors, increased human activity, and notable events have provided a critical moment in efforts for cybersecurity.

Examples of Security Programs

There are some effective and inexpensive Internet software programs (many with free trials) that can increase cybersecurity for websites and computers in general. Here is a list of some of the programs:

- AVG Secure Search
- AVG Internet Security
- Avast Free Antivirus 2015
- Norton Internet Security
- Comodo Antivirus 7
- Bitdefender Total Security 2015
- 360 Internet Security

What is HTML?

HTML stands for Hypertext Markup Language and is the primary language for web pages. It provides the structure and content of text-based information in a document. It also establishes certain text as links, headings, paragraphs, lists, etc. HTML is regarded as the foundation of all websites.

For example, HTML embeds images and objects, creates interactive forms, and establishes settings for headings, paragraphs, lists, links, etc. HTML instructs the web browser how to display a web page's words and images for the user. It is the responsibility of the web browser (i.e. Google Chrome, Internet Explorer, Firefox, etc.) to efficiently read HTML documents and displays them on the interface as web pages.

Tags

Each web page contains tags, which are commands inserted in a document that specifies how the document is formatted. Even though the browser does not display the HTML tags, it still uses the tags to determine how the content of the HTML page appears to the user.

HTML tags contain angle brackets like <>, and come in pairs, such as <> and </>. The first tag in the pair is called the start (or opening) tag, the second tag is the end (or closing) tag. The end tag appears similar to the start tag, but has a forward slash before the tag name.

Elements

An HTML element is defined as everything between the opening and closing tag, including all of the tags. Elements indicate to the browser how the HTML document is to be interpreted. More will be detailed about elements and tags in Chapter 2.

Attributes

An HTML attribute modifies the values an HTML element. HTML attributes appear as name-value pairs, which are separated by "=", and are in the start tag of an element, following the element's name:

An attribute is used to define and modify the characteristics of an HTML element and is placed inside the element's opening tag. All attributes are made up of two parts: a name and a value.

Attributes are commonly written in this form: **<tag attribute="value">(content modified by tag)</tag>.** Attribute values should be quoted; (even though it is not essential) leaving values unquoted can make the page unsafe.

Here is a table showing several common attributes used in HTML

Attribute	Purpose
align	Horizontally aligns tags on right, left, center
valign	Vertically aligns tags within an HTML element on the top, middle, bottom
bgcolor	Background color for page
background	Background image behind an element
width	Width of tables, images, or table cells.
height	Height of tables, images, or table cells.
title	Title of the elements (i.e. hyperlink).

The title attribute is used to attach an explanation to an element. It provides extra information about any element on a page. For instance, when you place your cursor over a hyperlink, a caption in a box displays. This attribute is referred to as a tooltip. It provides additional information and helps to expand on the meaning of the link. The anchor text names the link and the title text provides information about where the link will send the user. More information will be given about hyperlinks, anchor tags, and the title attribute in Chapter 3.

Example:

Look at a picture of a Tennessee highway below. The HTML is written as **<img src = "Tennessee(5).jpg" width = "200" height = "350" />.** The width and height are defined in pixels, and in the appropriate proportions to fit the page. They define the **<img>** element, which is modified by the source attribute (src). The source file is named **Tennessee(5).jpg.**

Chapter 2

Starting a Web Page

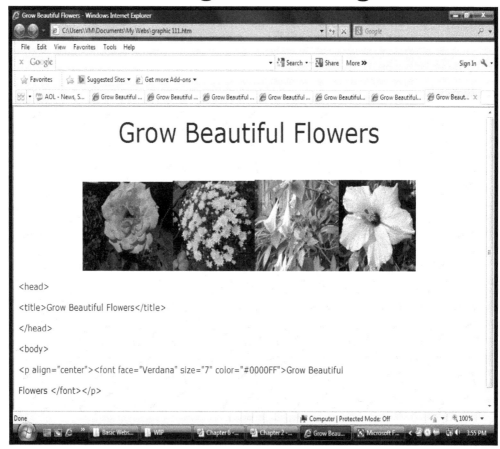

HTML Editors

An HTML editor is a specialized piece of software that enables the creation of HTML code. Users are able to enter raw text in order to create and maintain their websites. A good HTML editor helps boost productivity enormously. Here is a list of some of the most popular and effective editors:

- Microsoft Expression Web
- Google Web Designer
- Adobe Dreamweaver
- Microsoft Visual Web Developer
- Microsoft FrontPage
- Notepad

In this book, we will use Notepad to create the website.

Opening Notepad

1. Click Start Menu > All Programs > Accessories > Notepad.
2. Select the **Format** menu.
3. Click **Word Wrap**. This allows text to wrap on the screen.
4. Click on **Font**.

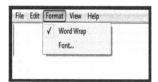

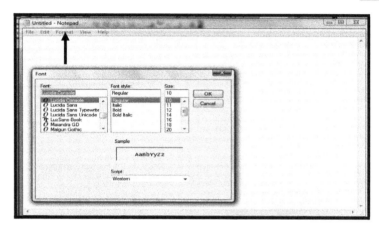

Selecting the Font

NOTE: The automatic font size in Notepad is 10pts, which may be too small for some users. To increase the font, font style, and size in Notepad:

1. Scroll down and click on **Lucinda Console** in the Font panel.
2. Click **Regular** in the **Font Style** panel.
3. Select 35 in the **Size** panel.

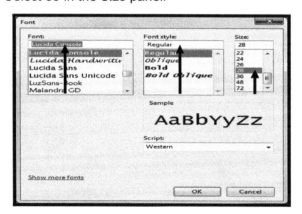

You have now setup the font style and size for the text on your web page. But before we continue, we will discuss the importance of elements and tags in HTML.

Elements

An HTML element is a component of an HTML document or web page. The HTML element encompasses all of the content located between the start tag and the end tag. Each element can have HTML attributes specified, with elements and text. Most elements are written with a start tag and an end tag, with the content in between. Elements include paragraphs, headings, anchor tags.

Example:

The title element or title tag, denoted as **<title>**, represents the title of the document that will display on a web browser.

When **<title>** Creation of a Website **</title>** is typed, the browser will display "Creation of a Website" when that page opens.

NOTE: There are six different heading tags, from largest to smallest are: **<h1>, <h2>, <h3>,<h4>, <h5>, and <h6>.** These tags determine the size of the font used in the heading

Here are some examples of HTML elements, with the start and end tags.

Elements (Start and end tag)	Element content
<h1></h1>....<h6></h6>	Heading 1...Heading 6
<p></p>	Paragraph
<html></html>	Defines the whole document
<a></a>	Anchor tag for hyperlink
 	Creates line breaks (does not need an end tag)
<body></body>	Document body

Adding Tags

In HTML, tags are added to text for development of the content of each web page. Think of tags as making your structure. Let's say you want a heading, you will put a tag at the exact point where it should start. Another tag is then needed where you want the heading to stop.

When creating a web page, you need to add tags according to special instructions. These tags will ensure that your text can be read in the web browser. Without tags in your text, your web page cannot be read.

Here is a list of common tags you will need:

<head>	Head	<h1>	Heading 1
<h2>	Heading 2	<h3>	Heading 3
<h4>	Heading 4	<h5>	Heading 5
<h6>	Heading 6	<title>	Title
<p>	Paragraph	<b>	Bold
<i>	Italic	<u>	underline

To continue building your web site:

1. Type **<html>** at the top of the screen.
2. Add **<head>** underneath the **<html>** tag, which refers to information about the document, such as the title and keywords that can be searched online.

3. Type **<title>** for the title of the website when it is opened in a web browser.

NOTE: In HTML each tag must be closed with an end tag which is a forward slash /
before the name of the tag. On the line with the **<title>** tag, put an end tag called
</title>. It is important that each tag is closed with an end tag.

4. Type Creation of a Website after the **<title>** tag
5. Add **</title>** which is the closing tag for the title **Creation of a Website**.

Your screen should look like this.

```
Example - Notepad
File Edit Format View Help
<html>
<head>
<title>Creation of a Website</title>
```

6. Press **ENTER** and add a **<body>** tag, on the next line. This tag provides for the structure and content to be displayed on the web page.

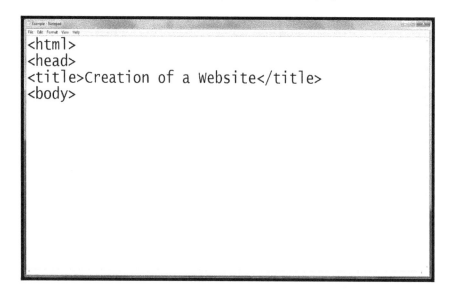

NOTE: You may notice that a closing </head> tag is not utilized in this book, because the pages function without them. I have found that the </head> tag could actually be considered optional. However, after the <title> and </title> tags, it is advisable to put a closing </head> tag, to ensure that website works efficiently.

Headings

You will now add a heading tag, which will give the size of the font for the heading on the page.

NOTE: There are six different heading tags, from largest to smallest: **<h1>, <h2>, <h3>,<h4>, <h5>, and <h6>.** For now we will choose **<h1>.**

1. Type the opening tag before the heading **<h1>Creation of a Website </h1>** the end tag.

```
<html>
<head>
<title>Creation of a Website</title>
<body>
<h1>Creation of a Website</h1>
```

2. Place the heading in the middle by adding a **<center>** tag after the **<h1>** tag and an end tag**</center>** before the **</h1>** tag.

Your Notepad screen should look like this:

```
<html>
<head>
<title>Creation of a Website</title>
<body>
<h1><center>Creation of a Website</h1></center>
```

Your screen should look like this

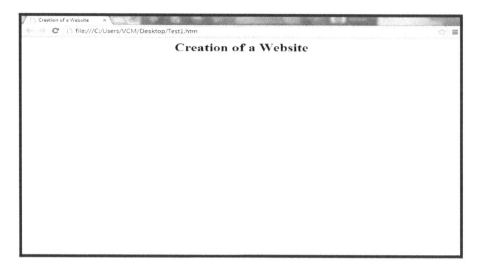

Adding Text

1. Add a **<p>** tag, which represents the paragraph where your text begins.
2. Type **<p>**This is an illustration of how to create a Web site. I will also illustrate how to use blogs and wikis.**</p>.**

Your screen should look like this:

```
<html>
<head>
<title>Creation of a Website</title>
<body>
<h1><center>Creation of a Website</h1></center>
<p>This is an illustration of how to create a Web site.
I will also illustrate how to use blogs and wikis.</p>
```

NOTE: You may continue to type as much text as you wish on the page when you are developing your website.

Pictures

Adding pictures makes it more appealing and expressive for the purpose of your website. But before adding a picture to the page, it is important to know the file type of the picture (what is the file extension).

- There are four image types that web pages use. These are the file types:
- GIF (Graphics Interchange Format)
- JPEG (Joint Photographic Experts Group)
- PNG (Portable Network Graphics)
- BMP (Bitmap)

To add a picture:

1. Place your cursor at the place you want your picture to show.
2. Type <img src = "Tennessee(5).jpg" width = "500" height = "350" />.

NOTE: If your picture does not display in the web page, retype the string of code and ensure that the file path is correct. To check for the file path, right click on the photo and select Properties to see the location of the file.

Your Notepad screen should look like this:

```
Example - Notepad
File  Edit  Format  View  Help
<html>
<head>
<title>Creation of a Website</title>
<body>
<h1><center><font size="7">Creation of a Website</h1></center>
</font>
<p>This is an illustration of how to create a
web site. I will also illustrate how to use blogs and wikis.
</font>
<img src = "Tennessee(5).jpg" width = "500" height = "350" /></a>
```

NOTE: You can use any width and height of the picture, depending on how large or small you want to make it. Remember to save the picture in the same folder as the web page.

Saving the File

1. Click File > Save As

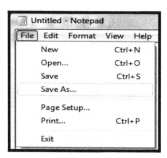

2. Save File Name as **Example.htm** on your desktop.

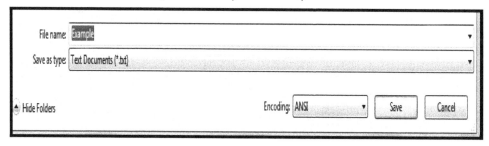

3. Look for where the file is saved and open it. Your web page will open in (Internet Explorer) or your default web browser.

Here is how it should look in your browser:

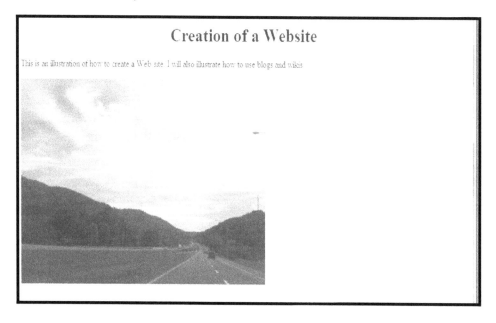

Changing the Font Size

1. Locate the file on desktop and double-click it.

NOTE: When creating a web page in Microsoft, the default web browser is the Internet Explorer. The font size in HTML is defined as any number from 1 to 6. The browser default size is 3. The font may look a bit too small for some users. We will change that by increasing the font size.

2. Type **<font size="6">.**
3. Type **</font></p>** on the next line.
4. Save file on desktop as **Example.htm**.
5. Locate file on desktop and open.

This is how the page looks now:

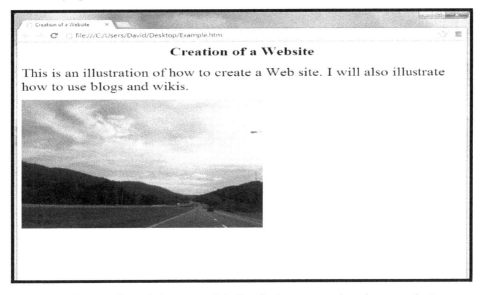

This is called the "Home Page", because it is the first page, and main page that appears on the site, and opens in the web browser. It is also the main page that all of the other pages link to and are organized around.

Adding Text to the Web Page

Type beneath the image tag **<p><font size="6">** Above is a picture of a Tennessee highway, taken on a road trip. This is an example of how a picture can appear on a web site.**</p></font>**

```
<html>
<head>
<title>Creation of a Website</title>
<body>
<h1><center>Creation of a Website</h1></center>
<p><font size="6">This is an illustration of how to create a
Web site. I will also illustrate how to use blogs and wikis.
</font></p>
<img src = "Tennessee(5).jpg" width = "500" height = "350" />
<p><font size="6">Above is a picture of a Tennessee highway,
taken on a road trip. This is an example of how a picture
can appear on a Web site.</p></font>
```

2.. Save file as **Example.htm**.

3.. Locate file on desktop and open it.

Here is the page now:

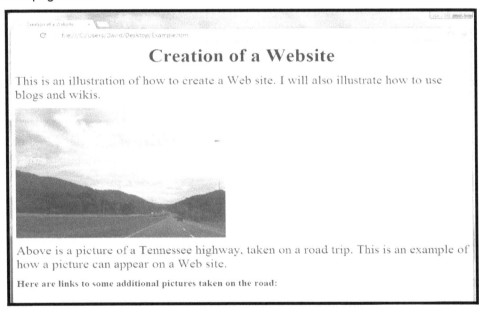

Check Your Progress

Part 1 - Font Size

1. Change the font size for the heading in **Example.htm**.
2. Open Example.htm.
3. On the line with **<h1>**Creation of a Website<center> add **<font size="7">.**
4. Add the closing **</font>** tag at the end of the paragraph or on another line.

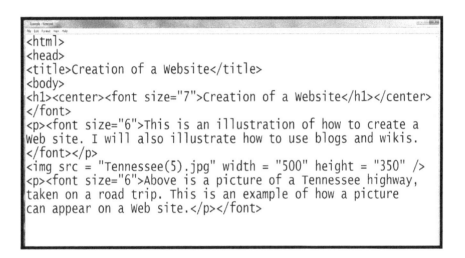

5. Save file as **Example.htm** on your desktop.
6. Locate and open the file.

Here is the page, with the increased heading size:

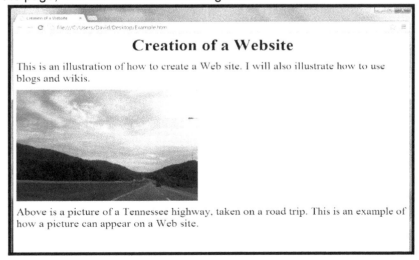

Part 2 - Headings

Now we will work with another heading: **<h2>**

1. Open Example.htm.
2. Scroll to where all of the text ends.
3. Type **<h2>**Here are links to some additional pictures taken on the road:**</h2>**.

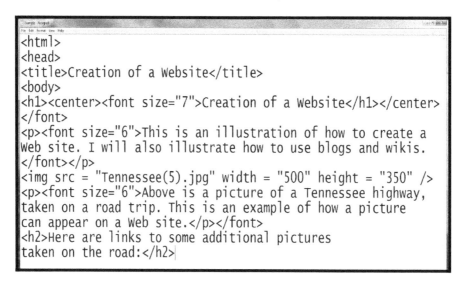

4. Save file as **Example.htm** on your desktop.
5. Locate the file and open it.

Here the file with the **<h2>** heading. That heading will be of specific use in the next chapter.

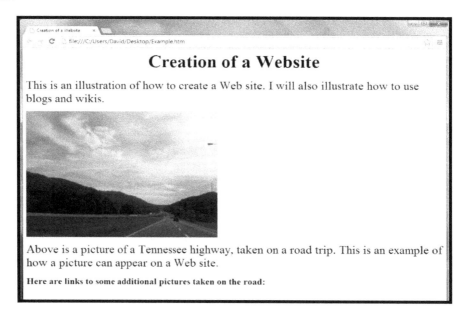

Part 3 -Title Attribute on a Picture

1. Open Example.htm
2. Scroll to the **<img src>** tag with Tennessee. After **height = "350"**, add title = **"Tennessee"**.

```
e</title>

Creation of a Website</h1></center>

n illustration of how to create a
trate how to use blogs and wikis.

g" width = "500" height = "350" title = "Tenneesse"/></a>
a picture of a Tennessee highway,
is an example of how a picture
o></font>
lick on the picture to access Google.</p></font>
additional pictures
```

3. Save as **ExamplePicAtt.htm** on your desktop
4. Locate and open the file.

When you mouse over the picture, the title attribute displays, showing the caption **"Tennessee"**.

Chapter 3

Adding Web Pages

Creating a Link

Links

A hyperlink can be a word, phrase, sentence, or an image that users can click on to jump to a new document or section within the current document. Hyperlinks are found in nearly all web pages, allowing users to navigate from page to page. With hyperlinks, information can be browsed and located instantly. Furthermore, links can be created on websites to audio, video and other web sites or pages. Hyperlinks are considered to be a highly essential ingredient of the World Wide Web.

Hyperlink Tags

To create a link, you have to add an anchor tag.

- The anchor tag or **<a>** tag is given that name because it is used for anchoring (i.e. connecting) links to another page in the same website, or other websites.
- Anchor tags also place links in the body of page. For hyperlinks, the **<a>** tag commonly contains **href,** which identifies where the link is targeted to (written as **<a href=...>).** Href stands for hypertext reference, which is the name of the file that is being linked.
- Additionally, the **href attribute** specifies the link's destination and specifies the URL of the page the link goes to.
- First create the page to which the link will go.

Below is an example of links on a web page:

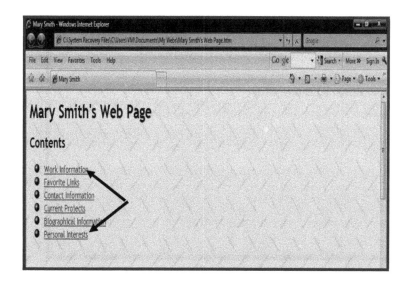

Creating the New Page

We will now create a page for Example.htm to link to.

1. Open **Notepad**.
2. Click Format > Font.
3. Select **Lucinda 36**.
4. Type **<html>** at the top of the screen.
5. Add **<head>** underneath the **<html>** tag.
6. Type **<title>** for the title of the page.
7. Type Downtown Atlanta after the **<title>** tag.
8. Close the title tag **</title>**.

The page should look like this:

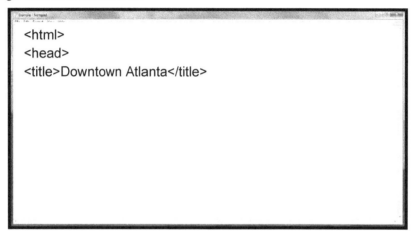

9. Type **<h1> Downtown Atlanta</h1> ** to place the heading in the center.

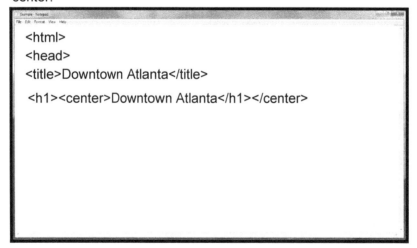

Adding a Photo

1. Place the cursor after the closed center tag and press **Enter**.
2. Type <p><font size="7">Here is a picture of my visit to Atlanta in 2012</p></font>.
3. Type <center><img src= DowntownATL.jpg" height ="400" width = "600" /></center>.

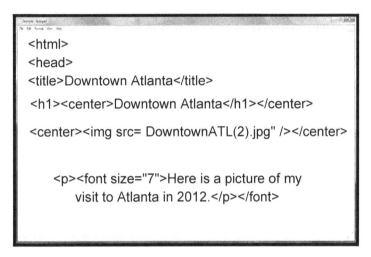

4. Save file as **DowntownATL.htm** on your desktop.
5. Locate and open the file.

Your page should look like this:

Linking to a Page

Now, we will create a hyperlink on Example.htm to the DowntownATL page.

1. Open Example.htm.
2. Beneath the description of the picture of a Tennessee highway, add the following: **<p><font size="6"> You can click on the picture to access Google</p></font>**.

NOTE: This indicates that the picture will be used as a link. We will discuss this further later in this chapter.

3. Scroll to <h2> Here are links to some additional pictures taken on the road:</h2> is located.
4. Place the cursor underneath the text and add a picture file by typing **<a href = "DowntownATL.htm">Downtown Atlanta</a>**.
5. Save the file as **Example.htm** on your desktop.
6. Locate and open the file.
7. Click on the **Downtown Atlanta** link on the DowntownATL page and it will open.

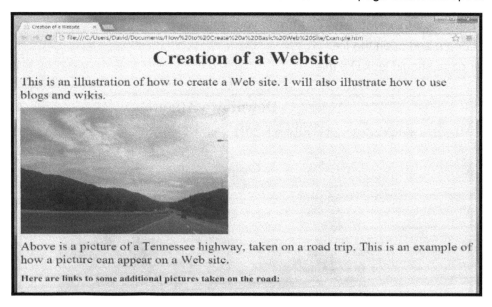

The hyperlink looks small. Let us make it bigger.

8. Scroll down to <a href="DowntownATL.htm">.
9. Add **<font size="5">** to the right of this tag.

```
<a href="DowntownATL.htm"><font size="5">Downtown Atlanta</a></font>
```

10. Add closing **</font>** tag at the end of the line.
11. Save as **Example.htm** on your desktop.
12. Locate and open the file.

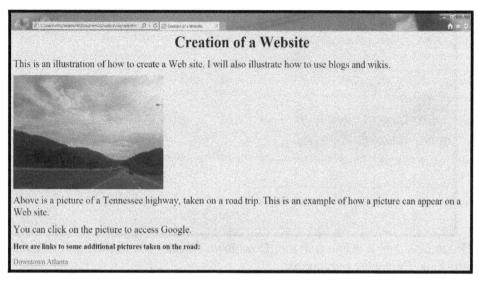

By linking the Downtown Atlanta page to the home page, we have begun the process of creating a website, with navigation.

Now let us try linking to another Web page:

1. Go to the "Creation of a Website" heading and title, and change it to Web Page.
2. Save the file as **Example1.htm**.
3. Locate and open **Example.htm**.
4. Type <a href= "Example1.htm"><font size="5">Page Link</a></font>.

```
<html>
<head>
<title>Creation of a Website</title>
<body>
<h1><center><font size="7">Creation of a Website</h1></center>
</font>
<p><font size="6">This is an illustration of how to create a
Web site. I will also illustrate how to use blogs and wikis.
</font></p>
<img src = "Tennessee(5).jpg" width = "500" height = "350" /></a>
<p><font size="6">Above is a picture of a Tennessee highway,
taken on a road trip. This is an example of how a picture
can appear on a Web site.</p></font>
<p><font size="6">You can click on the picture to access Google.</p></fon
<h2>Here are links to some additional pictures
taken on the road:</h2>
<a href="DowntownATL.htm"><font size="5">Downtown Atlanta</a></font>
<a href="Example1.htm"><font size="5">Page Link</a></font>
```

5. Save file as **Example.htm**.

6. Locate the file and open **Example.htm**.

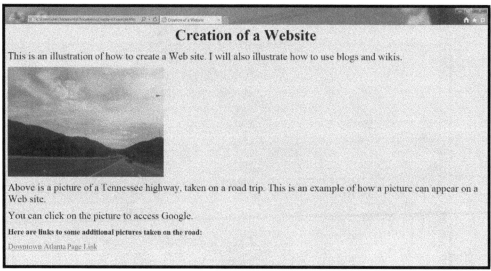

The "Page Link" link is in line with the "Downtown Atlanta" link to the right. When you click on Page Link, Example1.htm opens.

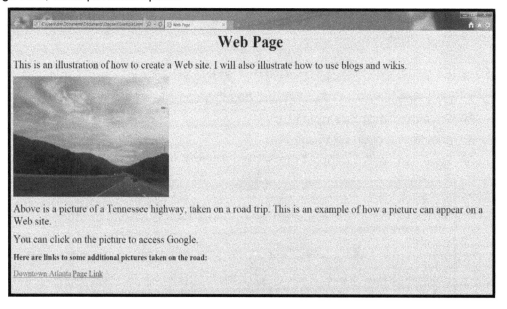

The title and heading for the page is Web Page. But the text and links are still the same. Let us change that.

To change the text in the links:

1. Locate **Example1.htm** on your desktop, and right-click on it.
2. Select Open With > Notepad.

3. Scroll to the line <p><font size="6">Above is a picture of a Tennessee highway, taken on a road trip. This is an example of how a picture can appear on a Web site.</p></font>

4. Replace "a Tennessee highway" with "Cincinnati", and "an" with "another".

5. Delete tag with "You can click on the picture to access Google."

6. Replace <img src = "Tennessee(5).jpg"…> with <img src = "Cincinatti.jpg" width = "500" height = "500" />.

7. Delete "This is an illustration of how…"

8. Save as **Example1.htm** on your desktop.

```
Example1 - Notepad
File  Edit  Format  View  Help
<html>
<head>
<title>Web Page</title>
<body>
<h1><center><font size="7">Web Page</h1></center>
</font>
<img src = "Cincinatti.jpg" width = "700" height = "500" />
<p><font size="6">Above is a picture of Cincinatti,
taken on a road trip. This is another example of how a picture
can appear on a web site.</p></font>
<h2>Here are links to some additional pictures
taken on the road:</h2>
<a href="DowntownATL.htm"><font size="5">Downtown Atlanta</a></font>
<a href="Example1.htm"><font size="5">Page Link</a></font>
```

9. Locate and open the file.

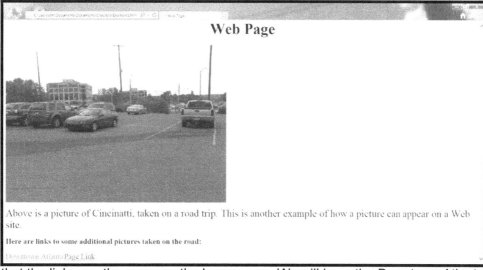

Above is a picture of Cincinatti, taken on a road trip. This is another example of how a picture can appear on a Web site.

Here are links to some additional pictures taken on the road:

Downtown Atlanta Page Link

Notice that the links are the same as the home page. We will keep the Downtown Atlanta link, but we will add a "Return Home" link, where the user can return to the home page.

To add the "Return Home" link:

1. Open Example1.htm.

2. Scroll down to the end of the page, and delete the tag for **Page Link**.

3. Type <p><center><a href="Example.htm"><font size="7">Return Home</a></font></p></center>.

```
<html>
<head>
<title>Web Page</title>
<body>
<h1><center><font size="7">Web Page</h1></center>
</font>
<img src = "Cincinatti.jpg" width = "700" height = "500" />
<p><font size="6">Above is a picture of Cincinatti,
taken on a road trip. This is another example of how a picture
can appear on a Web site.</p></font>
<h2>Here are links to some additional pictures
taken on the road:</h2>
<a href="DowntownATL.htm"><font size="5">Downtown Atlanta</a></font>
<p><center><a href="Example.htm"><font size="7">Return Home</a></font></p
```

4. Save as **Example1.htm** on your desktop.

5. Locate and open the file.

When you scroll down ......

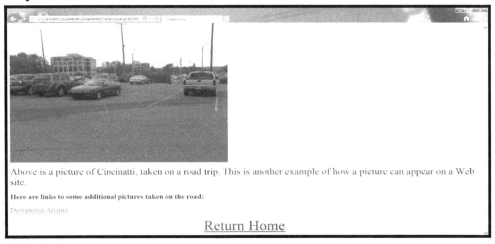

…you will see the **Return Home link**. The **<p>** tag, put the link on a different line, and the **<center>** tag put the link in the middle. The font size of 7 also made the link bigger. When you click on it, you will be taken back to the home page. This enhances the navigation and usability of the Web site.

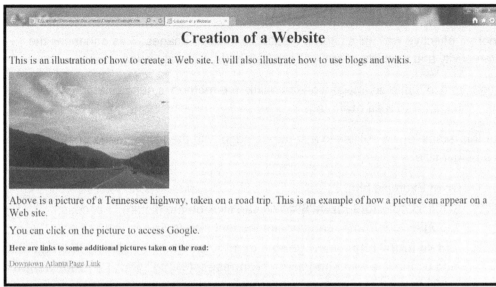

NOTE: To avoid having all of the files clutter the desktop, you can put the files in a folder, such as the one shown above. When I say "save the file on your desktop", putting the files on the desktop are really optional; you actually can put them in a folder. However, make sure and include all of the web files and picture files are in the same folder, for the website to fully function.

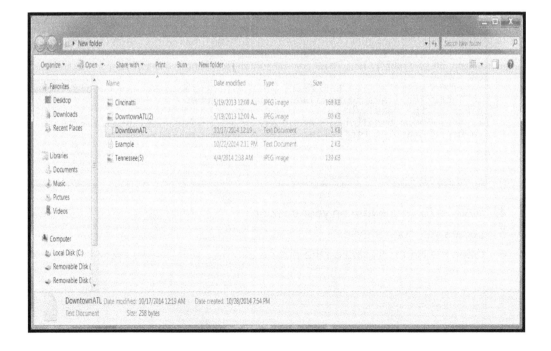

Using Images as Links

Another effective way links can be created is through images. This enhances the interactivity and usability of the website, rather than merely using text for links.

If you want to make an image work as a link, the method is quite similar to writing text for link. You start with a **<a href>** tag.

For this example, we will link to a separate page with the same image of Tennessee, but at a bigger size.

1. Open Example.htm.
2. Scroll **to <p><font size="6">**You can click on the picture to access **Google</p></font>,** and change the font size to 5.
3. Add **<a href="http://www.google.com">,** and then the closing **</a>** tag at the end on the line with **<img src = "Tennessee(5).jpg" width = "500" height = "350" />,**

```
Example - Notepad
File Edit Format View Help
<html>
<head>
<title>Creation of a Website</title>
<body>
<h1><center><font size="7">Creation of a Website</h1></center>
</font>
<p><font size="6">This is an illustration of how to create a
Web site. I will also illustrate how to use blogs and wikis.
</font></p>
<a href="http://www.google.com">
<img src = "Tennessee(5).jpg" width = "500" height = "350" /></a>
<p><font size="6">Above is a picture of a Tennessee highway,
taken on a road trip. This is an example of how a picture
can appear on a Web site.</p></font>
<p><font size="5">You can click on the picture to access Google.</p></for
<h2>Here are links to some additional pictures
taken on the road:</h2>
<a href="DowntownATL.htm"><font size="5">Downtown Atlanta</a></font>
<a href="Example1.htm"><font size="5">Page Link</a></font>
```

4. Save as **Example.htm** on your desktop
5. Locate and open the file.
6. Open the file by clicking on the picture.

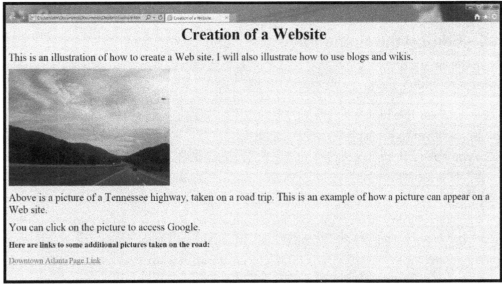

…you are taken to Google.

Check Your Progress

Part 1 - Editing the Home Page

Both hyperlinks are on the same line, and it likely looks confusing. So we will place them separate paragraphs, using a **<p>** tag:

1. Open Example.htm.
2. Scroll down to <a href="Example1.htm">.
2. Type <p><a href="Example1.htm"><font size="5">Page Link</a></font></p>.

```
Example - Notepad
File  Edit  Format  View  Help
<html>
<head>
<title>Creation of a Website</title>
<body>
<h1><center><font size="7">Creation of a Website</h1></center>
</font>
<p><font size="6">This is an illustration of how to create a
Web site. I will also illustrate how to use blogs and wikis.
</font></p>
<a href="http://www.google.com">
<img src = "Tennessee(5).jpg" width = "500" height = "350" /></a>
<p><font size="6">Above is a picture of a Tennessee highway,
taken on a road trip. This is an example of how a picture
can appear on a web site.</p></font>
<p><font size="5">You can click on the picture to access Google.</p></for
<h2>Here are links to some additional pictures
taken on the road:</h2>
<a href="DowntownATL.htm"><font size="5">Downtown Atlanta</a></font>
<p><a href="Example1.htm"><font size="5">Page Link</a></font></p>
```

5. Save the file as **Example.htm**.
6. Open and locate the file.

Now the links are on separate lines.

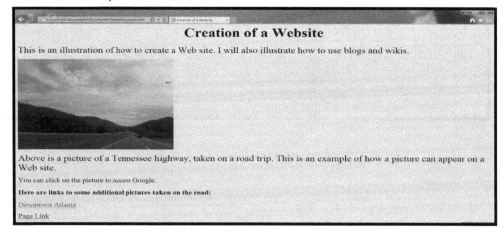

Part 2 – Title Attribute for Hyperlink

Now we will add a title attribute for hyperlinks.

1. Open Example.htm.
2. Scroll down to **<a href="Example1.htm">** and erase it.
3. Type <a href="DowntownATL.htm" title="Downtown ATL">.
4. Scroll down to **<p><a href="Example1.htm">** and erase it.
5. Type <p><a href="Example1.htm" title="Example1">.
6. Save as TitleExample.htm.

```
taken on the road.</h2>
<a href="DowntownATL.htm" title="Downtown ATL"><font size="5">Downtown At
<p><a href="Example1.htm" title="Example1"><font size="5">Page Link</a></
```

7. Locate and open the file.

Now when you open the file and place your cursor over the two links, the title attributes display.

Chapter 4

Other HTML Features

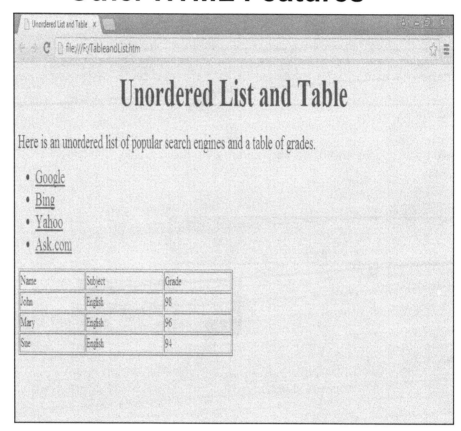

Managing Fonts

The font-face feature specifies the online fonts that display text on web pages. The face attribute specifies the font of the text inside a <font> element. The font-face also reduces reliance on the limited number of fonts that are installed on computers. It defines fonts, and influences the browser's selection of fonts. It is important to note that if the user viewing the page doesn't have the font installed, they will not be able to see it. Instead, the default font face applicable to the user's computer will appear.

Font face for custom fonts makes the page more searchable for users, when they want to find words on the page by using the Find (ctrl-F) feature. The text is more translatable via in-browser translation or translation services. When using a font face, the tag is commonly written with a coded set of letters and/or numbers. For example, if we wanted to use a red font, we would write <font color="#FFFFFF" face="Name of font" size="(Any number from 1 to 7)">. HTML color codes can be used to change the color of text, website backgrounds, tables, objects and images. The code must contain the tag # and six (6) numbers or letters. Here is a table of some font face color codes that can be used.

Font-face color code	Color
"#FFFF00"	Yellow
"#009933"	Green
"#FF0000"	Red
"#FF6600"	Orange
"#0000FF"	Blue
"#9933CC"	Purple
"#000000"	Black

Creating Backgrounds

The <body> background attribute creates a background image or color for HTML documents. Additionally, there is a tag for the body style with the background color setting. It is written as **<body style="background-color: (type of color)">.**

1. Open **Notepad**.
2. Type **<html>.**
3. Type **<head>.**
4. Type **<h1> <font color="#FFCC00" face="Verdana" size="7">Creation of a Web Page</h1> .**
5. Type **</head>.**
6. Type **<body><body style="background-color:green"><font color="#009933" face="Verdana" size="3">.**
7. Save file as **Website.html**.
8. Locate and open **Website.html**.

```
<html>
<head>
<title>Creation of a Website</title>
<h1><center><font color="#FFFF00"
face="Verdana" size="7">Creation of a
Website</h1></center></font>
<body><body style="background-
color:green"><font color="#009933"
face="Verdana" size="3">
```

This is an example of a website looks with a colored background, and colored font/heading.

Link this Page to Website.htm

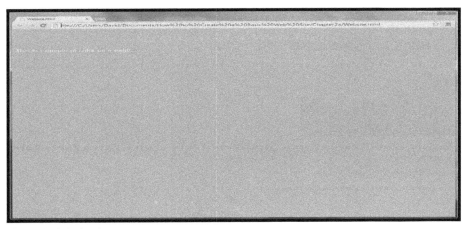

1. Open Website.htm.
2. Scroll down to the bottom of the page.
3. Type <p><a href="Website.htm"><font size="5">Website with Background</a></p>.
4. Save file as **Example.htm**.

```
<html>
<head>
<title>Creation of a Website</title>
<body>
<h1><center><font size="7">Creation of a Website</h1></center>
</font>
<p><font size="6">This is an illustration of how to create a
Web site. I will also illustrate how to use blogs and wikis.
</font></p>
<img src = "Tennessee(5).jpg" width = "500" height = "350" /></a>
<p><font size="6">Above is a picture of a Tennessee highway,
taken on a road trip. This is an example of how a picture
can appear on a Web site.</p></font>
<p><font size="5">You can click on the picture to access Google.</p></for
<h2>Here are links to some additional pictures
taken on the road:</h2>
<a href="DowntownATL.htm"><font size="5">Downtown Atlanta</a></font>
<p><a href="Example1.htm"><font size="5">Page Link</a></font></p>
<p><a href="Website.htm"><font size="5">Website with Background</a></p>
```

5. Locate and open the file.

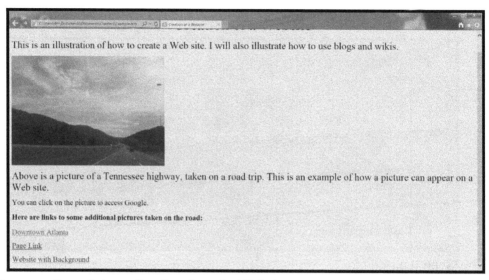

Now there are three links on the Creation of a Website page. However, if you click on the Website.htm link, the following screen appears.

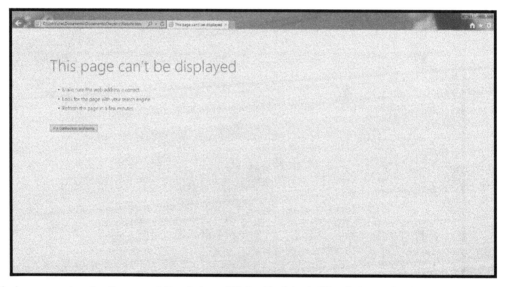

This is because I actually saved the link as **Website.html**. The link on the home page links to **Website.htm**.

1. Let us re-open Example.htm, and scroll down to the tag with **"Website with Background."**
2. Change from **Website.htm** to **Website.html**.
3. Save as **Example.htm** on your desktop.
4. Locate and open the file.

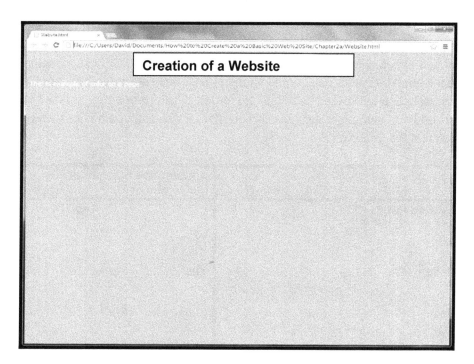

Now, when you click the **"Website with Background" link**, it opens the page. There is no real difference between **.htm** and **.html.** Both indicate that the file contains HTML. This is really an optional choice. In this case, I decided to go with .html. However, you have to make sure that the links not only match the files, but the extensions as well.

Generating Lists

HTML lists are bulleted lines of text that appear in the web browser in succession. HTML lists appear in web browsers as bulleted lines of text. There are three different types of HTML lists, including unordered lists (bullets), ordered lists (numbers), and definition lists (with bold headings, and plain text, a la dictionaries). Each list type has its own unique list tag, indicated in the table below.

Type of list	Appearance in Browser
Ordered list <ol> <li>item</li> <li>test2</li> </ol>	 Test1 Test2
Unordered list <ul> <li>test1</li> <li>test2</li> ….</ul>	 Test1 Test2
Definition list <dl> <dt>Definition</dt> <dd>This is a definition </dd> <dt>Another Definition</dt> <dd>This is another definition.</dd> </dt> </dl>	 Definition This is a definition. Another Definition This is another definition.

Example;

For this example, we will use an unordered list to describe different types of search engines (software that searches for data online).

1. Open **Notepad**.

2. Type the following text from this picture.

```
<html>
<head>
<title>List of Search Engines</title>
<body>
<h1><center><font size="7">List of Search Engines</h1></center>
</font>
<p><font size="6">Here is a list of popular search engines.
</font></p>
<ul>
    <li>Google</li>
    <li>Bing</li>
    <li>Yahoo</li>
    <li>Ask.com</li>
</ul>
```

3. Save as **SearchEngines.htm** on your desktop.

4. Locate and open the file.

Here is how the page looks:

Now we want to link it to the **Creation of a Website** home page.

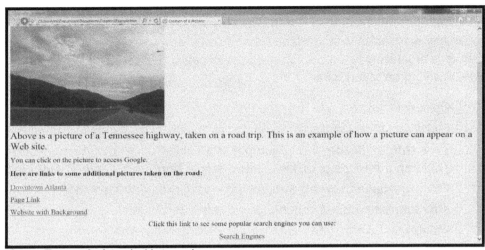

1. Open **Example.htm** in Notepad.
2. Scroll to the end of the page and type **<p><h2><font size="5"><center>Click this link to see some popular search engines you can use:</p></font>**.
3. Press Enter, then type **<p><a href="SearchEngines.htm"><font size="5">Unordered List</a></font></p></h2></center>**.
4. Save as **Example.htm** on your desktop.
5. Locate and open the file.

When you scroll down on the page, you will see the Unordered List link. However, this looks a bit bland, so let us open back up Example.htm in Notepad.

1. Open **Example.htm** in **Notepad**.
2. Scroll down to the **Unordered List** tag.
3. Replace **"Unordered List"** with **"Search Engines"**.

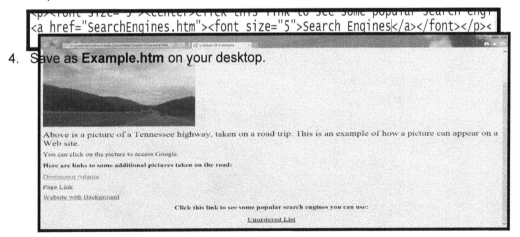

4. Save as **Example.htm** on your desktop.

Inserting Tables

Tables can easily be inserted in HTML websites using Notepad. You are able to create any number of columns and rows with the dimensions that you desire, You can also choose to create tables with or without borders on a web page. Tables are also very effective in organizing text and images on a web page. To insert a table with three columns and three rows on half of the web page:

1. Open your web page in Notepad
2. Place your cursor at the place where the table is to be inserted. Example:
3. Type **<html><head><title>Example of a Table</title><h1><center>Creating a Table on a Web page</h1></center><table border="1" style="width:50%"> <tr> <td>Name</td><td>Subject</td><td>Grade</td></tr><tr> <td>John</td><td> English</td><td>98</td></tr><tr> <td>Mary</td><td> English</td><td>96</td>></tr><tr> <td>Sue</td>td> English</td><td>94</td>></tr>**

This is how it looks in Notepad:

```
File  Edit  Format  View  Help
<html><head><title>Example of a Table</title>
<h1><center>Creating a Table on a Web
page</h1></center>
<table border="1" style="width:50%">
<tr><td>Name</td><td>Subject</td><td>Grade</td>
</tr><tr><td>John</td><td>
English</td><td>98</td></tr><tr><td>Mary</td>
<td>English</td><td>96</td></tr><tr><td>Sue</td
><td>English</td><td>94</td></tr>
```

This is how the table looks on the web page:

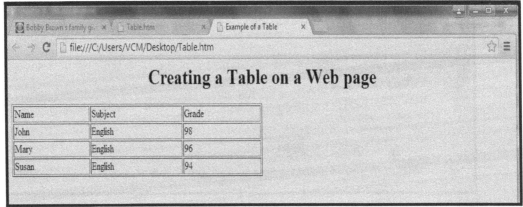

To insert a table with three columns and three rows to fill the entire width of the web page:

1. Open your web page in Notepad.
2. Place your cursor at the place where the table is to be inserted. The following is an example.
3. Type **<html><head><title>Example of a Table</title><h1><center>Creating a Table on a Web page</h1></center><table border="0" style="width:100%"> <tr> <td>Name</td><td>Subject</td><td>Grade</td></tr><tr> <td>John</td><td> English</td><td>98</td></tr><tr> <td>Mary</td><td> English</td><td>96</td>></tr><tr> <td>Sue</td>td> English</td><td>94</td>></tr>**

NOTE: For no table border, the dimension is "0" and for the width of the web page the dimension is 100%.

This is how the table looks without borders on the web page:

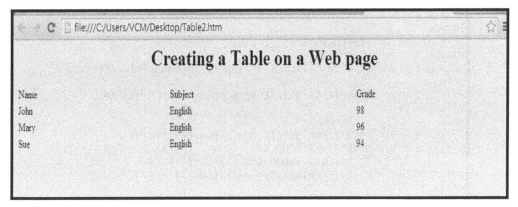

Check Your Progress

Part 1 - Adding links to Unordered Lists

Now that we have a page mentioning the popular search engines, for more interactivity and navigation, we should put each of the bulleted points as links, so that users can access those search engines.

1. Open **SearchEngines.htm** in Notepad.
2. Scroll down to the **<ul>** tag, and type what is displayed in the picture.

```
<html>
<head>
<title>List of Search Engines</title>
<body>
<h1><center><font size="7">List of Search Engines</h1></center>
</font>
<p><font size="6">Here is a list of popular search engines.
</font></p>
<ul>
  <li><a href="http://www.google.com">Google</li></a>
  <li><a href="http://www.bing.com">Bing</li></a>
  <li><a href="http://www.yahoo.com">Yahoo</li></a>
  <li><a href="http://www.ask.com">Ask.com</li></a>
</ul>
```

3. Save as **SearchEngines.htm** on your desktop.
4. Locate and open the file.

The user can click on each link and be taken to that particular search engine. For instance, when we click on the Bing link...

Part 2 – Bolding and Italicizing

In Chapter 2, the bold and italic font tags were introduced as the common tags you will need in HTM. Now, let us work with the bold and italic font tags on the search engines page.

1. Open SearchEngines.htm in Notepad.
2. Look for the line with <h1> <font size="7">List of Search Engines</h1> .
3. Type .
4. Scroll down to </ul> and press Enter.
5. Type the closing tags .

```
SearchEngines - Notepad

File  Edit  Format  View  Help
<html>
<head>
<title>List of Search Engines</title>
<body>
<h1><center><font size="7">List of Search Engines</h1></center><b><i>
</font>
<p><font size="6">Here is a list of popular search engines.
</font></p>
<ul>
   <li><a href="http://www.google.com">Google</li></a>
   <li><a href="http://www.bing.com">Bing</li></a>
   <li><a href="http://www.yahoo.com">Yahoo</li></a>
   <li><a href="http://www.ask.com">Ask.com</li></a>
</ul>
</b></i>
<p><center><a href="Example.htm"><font size="5">Return Home</a></font>
```

6. Save as SearchEngines.htm.

7. Locate and open the file.

The heading and the links are now bolded and italicized when viewed in a browser.

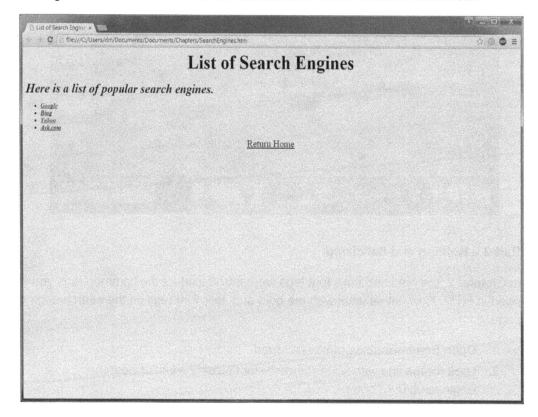

Chapter 5

Creating a Blog

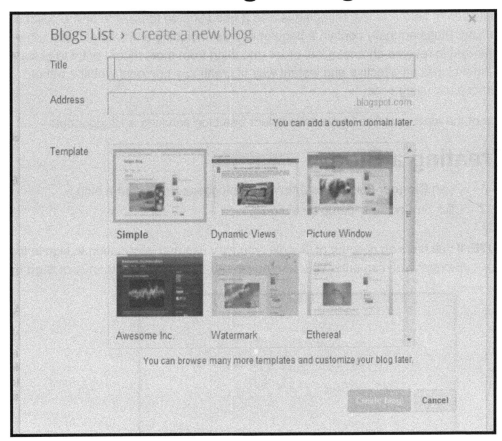

What is a Blog?

Weblogs (or blogs) are a collection of writings that can serve as portfolios for keeping record of personal content. They can be used in corporate and educational settings to track an individual's progress, serve as excellent tools for critiques, in addition to evaluation of performance. Blogging is also a good source to provide online collaborative learning. Blogs normally contain a page of entries, including archives of older entries, organized in reverse-chronological order (meaning from most recent entry to oldest). Using a blog is an effective and instant way of creating a personal website without methodically using code.

One of the most common and most efficient free blog services is Blogger.com.

Creating a Blog

1. Open **Blogger** homepage (http://www.blogger.com)to start a blog.
2. Click on **Create** to setup an account.

NOTE: If you have an account of Google, you may use that information to sign in to Blogger, you can enter your username and password, and then click **Sign in.**

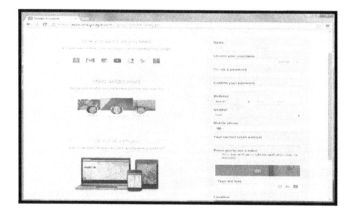

Add your name, username, password, e-mail address, birthday, gender and mobile phone number to help keep account secure.

NOTE: All Google accounts end with **@gmail.com.**

4. Fill in verification code, location, and then accept the **Terms of Service**.

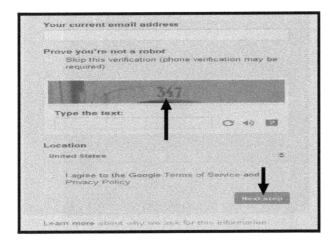

5. Click the **Create a Blog**, pick an address (URL) and a blog title.

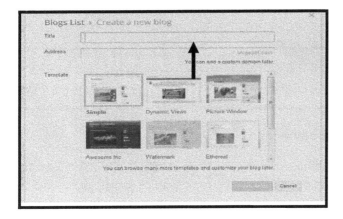

6. Select a blog template, which is how the blog will look once it is published.

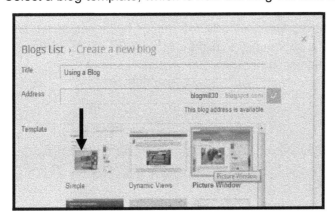

NOTE The title is **Using a Blog**, the address is **blogmill30.blogspot.com**, and the template selected is **Picture Window**.

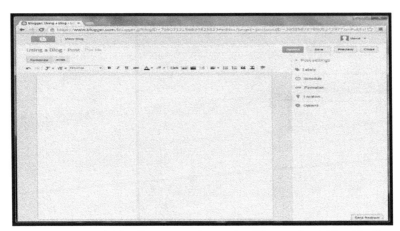

This screen appears which allows you to post a title, and add text to the page.

7. Click on Post Title, to type the title of the blog. The title of the post is **"What is a Discussion Board?"**

Add text (this text below) or compose your own:

A discussion board or threaded discussion is a forum in which instructors can post questions and announcements pertaining to the topic with readings, audio and video (Simonson et al., 2012). As a student, you can post comments and/or questions directed to instructors and fellow students on the discussion board, serving as further effective assessment tools of student performance and knowledge. The discussion boards used will come from Blackboard. The choice of your discussion topics has an effect on the quality and diversity of student responses and is usually determined by the instructor. Discussion boards will provide you with the opportunity to experience similar question/answer sessions as in face-to-face settings (Durrington, Berryhill, & Swafford, 2006). You will be able to create your own discussion posts on EDU 2.0.

References:

Durrington, V., Berryhill, A., & Swafford, J. (2006). Strategies for enhancing student interactivity in an online environment. College Teaching, 54(1), 190–193. Retrieved December 10, 2012
from http://www.redorbit.com/news/technology/433631/strategies_for_enhancing_student_interactivity_in_an_online_environment/

EDU 2.0 (2012). Features. Retrieved November 12, 2012
from http://www.edu20.org/info/features

Your post looks like this on the screen:

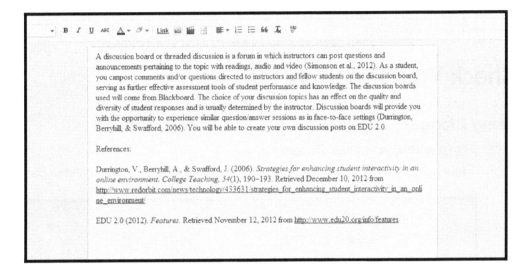

Publishing the Blog

1. Click on the **Publish** button.
2. Click on the **View Blog** button.

Here is how the blog looks:

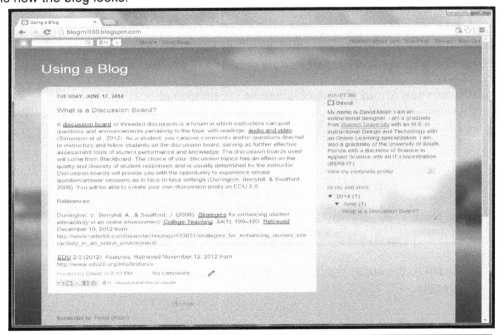

Check Your Progress

Using Blogger

1. Log-in to Blogger.com or Google.
2. Enter https://www.blogger.com/profile/00159416362139416940 in address bar.

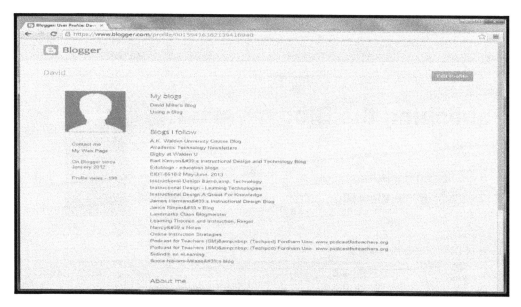

The list of **My Blogs** and **Blogs I Follow** appear.

You will also see **About Me**, which contains information about the user.

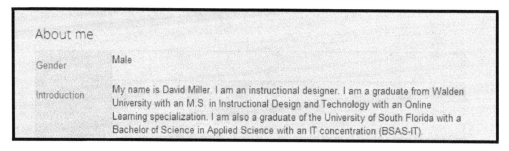

3. Scroll to the upper-right corner of the page and click on **Edit Profile**.

You will see **Edit User Profile** page, where you can edit and add information about privacy, identity, profile photo, audio, work and other personal information (interests, favorite movies, books, etc.).

4. Scroll down to the **Additional Information** section, and click on **Introduction**.

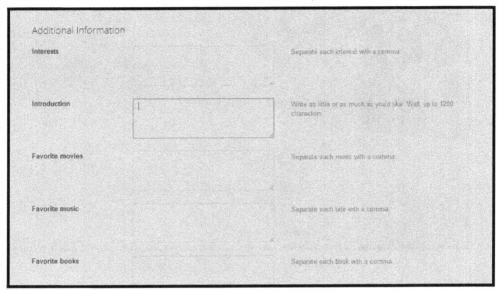

5. Add a brief introduction (1200 characters allowed) about yourself. Here is mine:

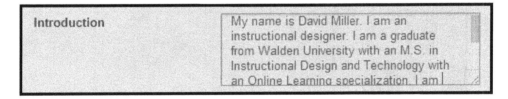

6. Scroll down and click **Save Profile**.
7. Scroll to the top of the screen, where there is a border saying **Your settings have been saved.**

8. Click on View Updated Profile.

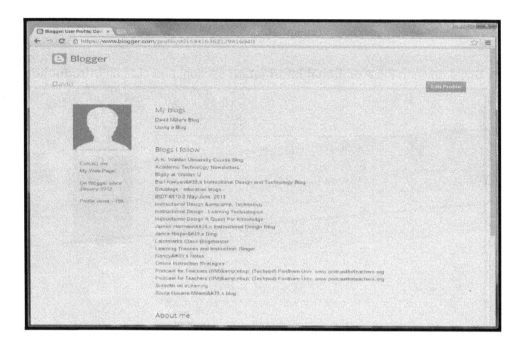

This is how the profile looks now.

9. Scroll down to **About me**, to see the description.

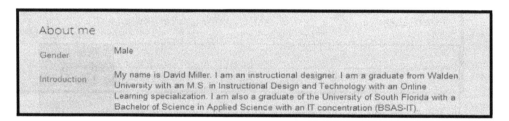

10. Scroll up to the **My blogs** section, and click on **Using a Blog**.

The blog http://blogmill30.blogspot.com/ appears.

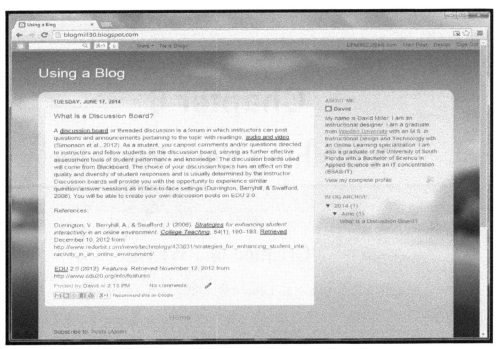

On the right corner, you will see About Me, and the description.

Now the profile is displayed on the blog.

Chapter 6

Publishing Your Website

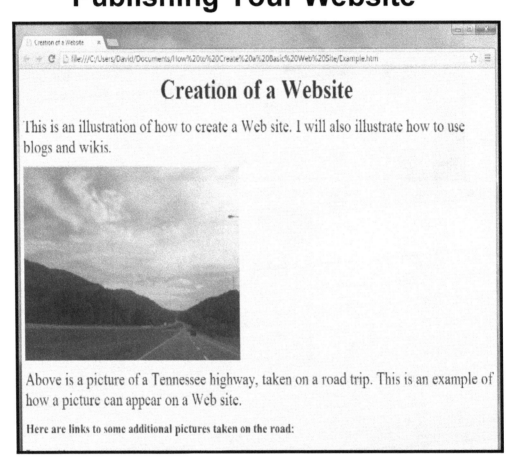

The Publishing Process

Once you have completed you website, the next step is to get it on the Internet so that you can make it available for visitors. The process of publishing your website involves the following steps:

- Choosing a domain name
- Selecting a hosting company
- Editing your web pages
- Maintaining your website

Choosing a Domain Name

The domain name identifies your website on the Internet. It should be as unique as possible, and not be similar to a popular site. It is important to keep in mind never to choose plurals of famous sites owned by others, intentionally misspelled version of any popular sites, or hyphenated versions of any popular domain name. Having domains with very similar names can lead to issues such as copyright infringement, and backlash by users. To avoid copyright issues, you should visit copyright.gov and look over some the rules and policies.

The domain name should be short enough for visitors to remember and type. Domains with shorter names are not only easier to remember, but also beneficial for visitors to tell others about the site. Irrelevant and clumsy characters such as hyphens, colons, and numbers should be avoided. Domain names need to be self-explanatory and indicative of what the website is presenting. Anyone hearing the domain name initially should have a decent idea of the contents on the site. This not only helps to attract more visitors, but also potential customers or business figures (if you are selling and marketing products and/or services). Each domain name ends with an extension which further defines the purpose of the website. Once you have decided on what your website presents you can choose an applicable extension. Here are some of the most commonly used extensions:

Extension	Purpose
.com	Used for businesses and commercial entities
.org	Used for organization, nonprofit groups and personal web pages
.net	Used mainly for technology based companies like web hosting services
.biz	Used for small business web sites

Selecting a Hosting Company

The final phase of creating a website is publishing your pages. To place your pages on the Web, you need a web server. Web servers allow you to transfer and store HTML documents and various multimedia files (audio, video, images, etc.). Choosing the best server depends on the type of site you want to maintain. Web sites fit into several categories: personal/hobby, business, social media, e-commerce, or e-businesses sites.

The website we have worked on fits into the category of a personal site, since it is basic in design and content. People use these types of sites to communicate with friends and family.

The size, complexity, and expected traffic load of your site are important things to consider when you go shopping for a host. To create a new website, the first thing to decide is on a name. See examples listed above. You want to look for a free or inexpensive web host company that offers services that meet the needs of your website. The level of hosting service depends on whether the website has multiple pages or has one page. Most hosting companies offer the same basic services such as email accounts; secure internet connectivity, website management portals and usage reports. Additionally, users can choose free domain hosting, which enables clients to host their own domain names on servers at no additional cost.

Web hosting is usually done on an annual basis and is renewable. Clients also have the option of signing on for one, two or three year contracts. Website hosting providers that such as HostGator, iPage, Dot5hosting, Hostmonster and JustHost offer relatively inexpensive hosting services, Providers offer a system for users to upload files through their web browser. It is important to note that for proper control of the site, FTP access is necessary. FTP means File Transfer Protocol, which is the way files are transferred from one computer to another. An FTP client program is needed for FTP access. Programs that can be used included Cute FTP and FileZilla. Microsoft FrontPage can be a useful and convenient FTP client program. When the address, username and password are setup you can use your FTP program to connect to your server.

Editing the Site

Editing Colors for your Site

When creating a site, choosing a proper color scheme is one of the most important factors. In other words, it is important to ensure that the text and background colors do not clash, which helps to effectively communicate the message of the site. The color scheme that you use on your website can entice the visitor to continue to read your site, as well as influence the visitor's decision whether to keep browsing your site. Users may opt to leave it because of a poor selection of colors and other visual elements. Create a strong contrast between a page's background and its text. The best and most basic combination for readability is a black text on white background. Other effective website background colors and text combinations are gray and black with white text, and green with yellow text.

Copy and pasting tags from different files

It is important to know about saving, copying and pasting, and creating backup files (in case there is anything that is forgotten). This not only applies for web pages, but for the computer in general.

1. Locate and open PictureExample.htm.
2. Right-click on it, and open in Notepad.
3. Scroll down to the last two links of the page.
4. From <a href=DowtownATL.htm…"> to the </p> tag, place your cursor and drag the mouse until all of those words are covered in blue.

```
PictureExample - Notepad
File  Edit  Format  View  Help
<html>
<head>
<title>Creation of a website</title>
<body>
<h1><center><font size="7">Creation of a website</h1></center>
</font>
<p><font size="6">This is an illustration of how to create a
web site. I will also illustrate how to use blogs and wikis.
</font></p>
<img src = "Tennessee(5).jpg" width = "500" height = "350" title = "Tenne
<p><font size="6">Above is a picture of a Tennessee highway,
taken on a road trip. This is an example of how a picture
can appear on a web site.</p></font>
<p><font size="5">You can click on the picture to access Google.</p></for
<h2>Here are links to some additional pictures
taken on the road:</h2>
<a href="DowntownATL.htm" title="Downtown ATL"><font size="5">Downtown At
<p><a href="Example1.htm"><font size="5">Page Link</a></font></p>
```

5. Right-click and select Copy.

6. Open Example.htm.

7. Similar to the actions in PictureExample.htm, block off from `<a href...>` to `</p>` on the second line. Right-click, but this time, select Paste.

```
<html>
<head>
<title>Creation of a website</title>
<body>
<h1><center><font size="7">Creation of a website</h1></center>
</font>
<p><font size="6">This is an illustration of how to create a
web site. I will also illustrate how to use blogs and wikis.
</font></p>
<img src = "Tennessee(5).jpg" width = "500" height = "350" /></a>
<p><font size="6">Above is a picture of a Tennessee highway,
taken on a road trip. This is an example of how a picture
can appear on a web site.</p></font>
<p><font size="5">You can click on the picture to access Goog
<h2>Here are links to some additional pictures
taken on the road:</h2>
<a href="DowntownATL.htm"><font size="5">Downtown Atlanta</a>
<p><a href="Example1.htm"><font size="5">Page Link</a></font></p>
<p><a href="Website.html"><font size="5">Website with Background</a></for
<p><font size="5"><center>Click this link to see some popular search engi
<a href="SearchEngines.htm"><font size="5">Search Engines</a></font></p><
```

Now, the title attribute is added to the Downtown ATL link.

```
<head>
<title>Creation of a website</title>
<body>
<h1><center><font size="7">Creation of a website</h1></center>
</font>
<p><font size="6">This is an illustration of how to create a
web site. I will also illustrate how to use blogs and wikis.
</font></p>
<img src = "Tennessee(5).jpg" width = "500" height = "350" /></a>
<p><font size="6">Above is a picture of a Tennessee highway,
taken on a road trip. This is an example of how a picture
can appear on a web site.</p></font>
<p><font size="5">You can click on the picture to access Google.</p></fon
<h2>Here are links to some additional pictures
taken on the road:</h2>
<a href="DowntownATL.htm" title="Downtown ATL"><font size="5">Downtown At
<p><a href="Example1.htm"><font size="5">Page Link</a></font></p>
<p><a href="Website.html"><font size="5">Website with Background</a></fon
<p><font size="5"><center>Click this link to see some popular search engi
<a href="SearchEngines.htm"><font size="5">Search Engines</a></font></p><
```

However, our work is not complete...

1. Locate and open TitleExample.htm.
2. Scroll down to **\<p>\<a href="Example1.htm" title="Example1">\<font size="5">Page Link\</a>\</font>\</p>.**

```
of a Website</title>

t size="7">Creation of a Website</h1></center>

">This is an illustration of how to create a
 also illustrate how to use blogs and wikis.

essee(5).jpg" width = "500" height = "350" /></a>
">Above is a picture of a Tennessee highway,
trip. This is an example of how a picture
web site.</p></font>
">You can click on the picture to access Google.</p></font>
ks to some additional pictures.
d:</h2>
hATL.htm" title="Downtown ATL"><font size="5">Downtown Atlanta</a></font>
ple1.htm  title="Example1"><font size="5">Page Link</a></font></p>
```

3. Drag mouse and block off the entire line.
4. Right click, and select Copy.
5. Go back to Example.htm.
6. Scroll down to **\<p>\<a href="Example1.htm" title="Example1">\<font size="5">Page** Link\</a>\</font>\</p>.

```
taken on the road:</h2>
<a href="DowntownATL.htm" title="Downtown ATL"><font size="5">Downtown At
<p><a href="Example1.htm"><font size="5">Page Link</a></font></p>
<p><a href="Website.html"><font size="5">Website with Background</a></for
<p><font size="5"><center>Click this link to see some popular search engi
<a href="SearchEngines.htm"><font size="5">Search Engines</a></font></p><
```

7. Block off the entire line.
8. Right-click and select Paste.

```
    <p><a href="Example1.htm" title="Example1"><font size="5">Page Link</a></
    <p><a href="Website.html"><font size="5">Website with Background</a></for
```

Now the Example1.htm link has the title attribute.

Next, put additional title attributes to the Tennessee picture tag and Search Engines tag. Make sure they respectively look like the following:

\<img src = "Tennessee(5).jpg" width = "500" height = "350" title = "Tennessee"/>\</a>

\<a href="SearchEngines.htm" title="Search Engines">\<font size="5">Search Engines\</a>\</font>\</p>\</center>

Maintaining your Website

Owning a website requires primary responsibilities of maintenance, monitoring and content updates. The host company ultimately does not monitor the upkeep of your website. You, as the webmaster (the person who has created, designed and manages the website) are responsible for that. Successful websites require continuous maintenance so it can attract users and/or customers if your site is used to provide goods and services. This is akin to maintaining your home, or a paper or book being written. It is a constant work in progress. Regular website maintenance enables your site to run smoothly. It is suggested that users should schedule at least a monthly checkup. In my opinion, websites should be checked at least twice a week, to keep visitors updated and interested. It is also important to check the links frequently. Links become broken over time or due to bugs from the computer and server. Brokenlinkcheck.com is free and can detect which of the hyperlinks don't work, and where exactly the problems are located in the HTML code. All that has to be done is to type the website address in the "Free Check for Broken Links" box.

Because websites are subject to being hacked, you can avoid this from happening by keeping the files up to date. Backing up your website should be done often. Though web hosting companies state that they backup the sites on their servers, their backup may not include your last edit. If the server crashes, someone hacks into the site, or if files get deleted, the edits will be gone, and the hosting company will only restore what they had backed up initially. A whole day's work could be lost because you did not backup the site. All of the website files should be kept on media such as flash drives and/or CDs. Because creating and designing a website is a work in progress, copies of files, or "testing" files should be created and saved, until you are satisfied with your site, and it is working properly.

Appendix 1

Template for a Personal Web Page in HTML

1. Copy the HTML code into Notepad.
2. Change the font size on the Format menu.
3. Enter your personal information.
4. Save the file as a text file on your Desktop- Example – Personal1.txt
5. Save the file with an .htm file extension. Example – Personal2. htm
6. Open the HTML file. It will display in your browser.
7. Make any changes and repeat #2 and #3.

```
<head>

<body>

<h1>Your name Web Page</h1>

<h2>Contents</h2>

 <li><a href="#_Work_Information">Work Information</a>

 <li><a href="#_Favorite_Links">Favorite Links</a>

 <li><a href="#_Contact_Information">Contact Information</a>

 <li><a href="#_Current_Projects">Current Projects</a>

 <li><a href="#_Biographical_Information">Biographical Information</a>

 <li><a href="#_Personal_Interests">Personal Interests</a></li>

</ul>

<p class="MsoNormal"><o:p>

</p>

<h2><a name="_Work_Information"></a>Work Information</h2>

<h3>Job Title</h3>

<p class="MsoNormal">Type some text.</p>

<h3>Key responsibilities</h3>
```

```
<p class="MsoNormal">Type some text.</p>

<h3>Department or workgroup</h3>

<p class="MsoNormal">Type some text.</p>

<p class="MsoNormal"></p>

</p>

<a href="#_top">Back to top</a></p>

<h2><a name="_Favorite_Links"></a>Favorite Links</h2>

  <li>Insert a hyperlink here

  <li>Insert a hyperlink here

  <li>Insert a hyperlink here</li>

</ul>

</p>

<p class="MsoNormal"><a href="#_top">Back to top</a></p>

<h2><a name="_Contact_Information"></a>Contact Information</h2>

<h3>E-mail address</h3>

<p>Type some text.</p>

<h3>Web address</h3>

<p>Type some text.</p>

<h3>Office phone</h3>

<p>Type some text.</p>

<p><a href="#_top">Back to top</a></p>

<h2><a name="_Current_Projects"></a>Current Projects</h2>

  <li>Insert project title

  <li>Insert project title

  <li>Insert project title</li>

</ul>
```

```
<p><a href="#_top">Back to top</a></p>

<h2><a name="_Biographical_Information"></a>Biographical Information</h2>

<p>Type some text.</p>

<p><a href="#_top">Back to top</a></p>

<h2><a name="_Personal_Interests"></a>Personal Interests</h2>

  <li>Add an interest

  <li>Add an interest

  <li>Add an interest</li>

</ul>

</p>

<p><a href="#_top">Back to top</a></p>

<p>Last revised: Date</p>

</body>

</html>
```

Appendix 2

References

Alimoqi (2011). Optional Closing Tags in HTML. [Online discussion group]. Retrieved from http://www.neowin.net/forum/topic/978214-optional-closing-tags-in-html/

Amin, T. (2014). Importance of a great domain name. Retrieved from

https://www.linkedin.com/pulse/20140418111410-15451038-importance-of-a-perfect-domain-name

Avangate. Choosing the Right Colors for Your Web Site. Retrieved from http://www.avangate.com/avangate-resources/article/color-web-site.htm

Avast (2015). Retrieved from https://www.avast.com/en-us/index

AVG (2014). Retrieved from http://www.avg.com/us-en/internet-security

AVG (2014). AVG Secure Search. Retrieved from http://www.avg.com/us-en/secure-search

AVG (2014). Company Profile. Retrieved from http://www.avg.com/us-en/avg-company-profile

Barnes, V. Where Do I Put My Website? Retrieved from http://www.htmlgoodies.com/introduction/intro/article.php/3473581

Brain, M. How Blogs Work. Retrieved fromhttp://computer.howstuffworks.com/internet/social-networking/information/blog.htm

Burns, J. Web Developer Class: Learn the Basic HTML Tags! Retrieved fromhttp://www.htmlgoodies.com/primers/html/article.php/3478151

Computer Hope (2014). E-Mail. Retrieved from http://www.computerhope.com/jargon/e/email.htm

Computer Hope (2014). Address bar. Retrieved from http://www.computerhope.com/jargon/a/addrebar.htm

ConsumerRankings.com (2014). Our Best Web Hosting Picks of 2014. Retrieved from http://www.consumer-rankings.com/hosting-

reviews/?a=148&c=2968&s1=55220166.58806851&ls=g&gclid=CPu4h4rrl74CFePm7Aod
yBYAQA

Download.com (2014). Avast Internet Security 2015 Retrieved from
http://download.cnet.com/Avast-Internet-Security-2015/3000-18510_4-75095376.html

Download.com (2014). Internet Security Software Suites for Windows. Retrieved from
http://download.cnet.com/windows/internet-security-software-suites/

Dragon13304 (2013). Best Web Browsers
Retrieved from http://www.thetoptens.com/best-web-browsers/

EchoEcho.com. Image Links.
Retrieved from http://www.echoecho.com/htmllinks06.htm

Evoch.com. What is the difference between the HTM and HTML extensions?
Retrieved from http://www.sightspecific.com/~mosh/www_faq/ext.html

Fogarty, M. (2010). Capitalizing Proper Nouns. Retrieved from
http://www.quickanddirtytips.com/education/grammar/capitalizing-proper-nouns

Gold, L. (2010). AP Stylebook surrenders the battle over "Web site" vs. "website".
Retrieved from https://lisagoldresearch.wordpress.com/2010/04/17/ap-stylebook-
surrenders-the-battle-over-web-site-vs-website/

Google. Blogger Getting Started Guide. Retrieved
fromhttps://support.google.com/blogger/answer/1623800?hl=en

Grammarist. Website vs. web page. Retrieved from http://grammarist.com/usage/website-
web-page/

Herrod, S. (2015). The Cybersecurity Tipping Point. Retrieved from
http://techcrunch.com/2015/01/02/the-cybersecurity-tipping-point/

HTML5 Rocks. Quick guide to webfonts via @font-face. Retrieved from
http://www.html5rocks.com/en/tutorials/webfonts/quick/

HTML Color Codes (2012). HTML Color Codes. Retrieved from http://html-color-
codes.info/

HTML Goodies Staff. How To Change Text Color Using HTML and CSS. Retrieved from
http://www.htmlgoodies.com/tutorials/colors/article.php/3479011

IBM. The Rise of the Internet. Retrieved from http://www-03.ibm.com/ibm/history/ibm100/us/en/icons/internetrise/

Immigration-usa.com. Complete HTML True Color Chart. Retrieved from http://www.immigration-usa.com/html_colors.html

Internet Society (2014). Brief History of the Internet.
Retrieved from http://www.internetsociety.org/internet/what-internet/history-internet/brief-history-internet

Itegrity. Website Maintenance- How to Maintain Your Website After You Launch It!
Retrieved from http://www.itegritygroup.com/website-maintenance/

Merriam-Webster (2014). Search Engine. Retrieved from http://www.merriam-webster.com/dictionary/search%20engine

Mozilla Developer Network (2014). @font-face.
Retrieved from https://developer.mozilla.org/en-US/docs/Web/CSS/@font-face

MyWebServices (2014). Difference between intranet & extranet. Retrieved from http://www.mywebservices.ca/diff_intranet_extranet.html

New Perspectives on the Internet, Fifth Edition, Brief, 5th Edition
Schneider/Evans - ©2004
http://browsers.about.com/od/howbrowserswork/a/whatisabrowser.htm

Online Broken Link Checker (2015).
Retrieved from http://www.brokenlinkcheck.com/

Page Rank Checker (2012). Top 10 Free Web Hosting sites.
Retrieved from http://www.prchecker.info/web-hosting/top-10-free-web-hosting-sites/

Rubenking, N.J. (2014). The Best Free Antivirus for 2015. Retrieved from http://www.pcmag.com/article2/0,2817,2388652,00.asp

Shannon, R. (2012). Uploading your Site. Retrieved from http://www.yourhtmlsource.com/myfirstsite/uploading.html

Shareware on Sale (2015). Free AVG Internet Security 2015 (100% discount)
Retrieved from http://sharewareonsale.com/s/free-avg-internet-security-2014-54-99-value

Sitepoint. @font-face.
Retrieved from http://reference.sitepoint.com/html/font/size

SitePoint. size (HTML attribute). Retrieved from http://reference.sitepoint.com/css/at-fontface

Sitepoint. Title (HTML attribute). Retrieved from http://reference.sitepoint.com/html/core-attributes/title

Softonic (2014). Avast Free Antivirus 2015. Retrieved from
http://avast.en.softonic.com/

Smarty, A. How to Use Link TITLE Attribute Correctly. Retrieved from
http://www.searchenginejournal.com/how-to-use-link-title-attribute-correctly/

Smith, B. How to Create a Simple Table on Your Web Page. Retrieved from
http://www.dummies.com/how-to/content/how-to-create-a-simple-table-on-your-web-page.html

Sprint (2013). Milestone Events Making Sprint History: 1899 – 1989. Retrieved from
http://www.sprint.com/companyinfo/history/

PageResource. Using an Image as a Link. Retrieved from
http://www.pageresource.com/html/image3.htm

Portable Network Graphics. Retrieved from http://www.libpng.org/pub/png/

TechTerms.com. Hyperlink. Retrieved from http://www.techterms.com/definition/hyperlink

TechTerms.com. Wiki. Retrieved from http://www.techterms.com/definition/wiki

The Cheat Vault. YouTube color codes. Retrieved from
http://thecheatvault.weebly.com/youtube-color-codes.html

The Chicago Manual of Style. Significant Rule Changes in The Chicago Manual of Style, 16th Edition. Retrieved from http://www.chicagomanualofstyle.org/about16_rules.html

The Spotted Dog Bed and Breakfast. Retrieved from
http://www.willcam.com/cmat/html/crossname.html

Thomason, L (2002). Beginner Tip: Publishing Your Web Page, Part 1. Retrieved from
http://www.netmechanic.com/news/vol5/beginner_no24.htm

Tizag.com. HTML Tutorial – Lists. Retrieved from http://www.tizag.com/htmlT/lists.php

Trapani, G (2005). Geek to Live: How to set up a personal home web server. Retrieved from http://lifehacker.com/124212/geek-to-live--how-to-set-up-a-personal-home-web-server

TutorialsPoint. HTML Attributes. Retrieved from
http://www.tutorialspoint.com/html/html_attributes.htm

TutorialsPoint (2014). HTML Fonts. Retrieved from
http://www.tutorialspoint.com/html/html_fonts.htm

Tutorial Resource Centre. Adding More Pages Using Links. Retrieved from
http://www.resource-centre.net/html-using-links-and-anchors

Typepad Knowledge Base (2014). Add Anchor Tags To Jump To Specific Location On A Page. Retrieved from http://help.typepad.com/anchor-tags.html

w3schools.com. HTML <a> name Attribute.Retrieved from http://www.w3schools.com/tags/att_a_name.asp

w3schools.com. HTML <body> background Attribute. Retrieved from http://www.w3schools.com/tags/att_body_background.asp

w3schools.com. HTML <font> face Attribute. Retrieved from http://www.w3schools.com/tags/att_font_face.asp

w3schools.com. HTML <source> src Attribute. Retrieved from http://www.w3schools.com/tags/att_source_src.asp

w3schools.com. HTML Introduction. Retrieved from http://www.w3schools.com/html/html_intro.asp

Webopedia. Hyperlink. Retrieved from http://www.webopedia.com/TERM/H/hyperlink.html

Webopedia. Tag. Retrieved from http://www.webopedia.com/TERM/T/tag.html

Web Page Mistakes. Backing Up Your Website. Retrieved from http://www.webpagemistakes.ca/backing-up-your-website/

Whatis.com (2006). Webmaster. Retrieved from http://whatis.techtarget.com/definition/Webmaster

Wikipedia (2014). Blog. Retrieved from http://en.wikipedia.org/wiki/Blog

Wikipedia (2014). History of the Internet. Retrieved from http://en.wikipedia.org/wiki/History_of_the_Internet

Wikipedia (2014). HTML. Retrieved from http://en.wikipedia.org/wiki/HTML

Wikipedia (2014). Internet Security. Retrieved from http://en.wikipedia.org/wiki/Internet_security

Wikipedia (2014). List of HTML editors. Retrieved from http://en.wikipedia.org/wiki/List_of_HTML_editors

Wikipedia (2014). Web navigation. Retrieved from http://en.wikipedia.org/wiki/Web_navigation

Wikipedia (2014). World Wide Web. Retrieved from http://en.wikipedia.org/wiki/World_Wide_Web

w3schools.com. HTML <a> Tag. Retrieved from http://www.w3schools.com/tags/tag_a.asp

w3schools.com. HTML
 Tag. Retrieved from
http://www.w3schools.com/tags/tag_br.asp

w3schools.com. HTML <img> height Attribute. Retrieved from
http://www.w3schools.com/tags/att_img_height.asp

w3schools.com. HTML Elements. Retrieved from
http://www.w3schools.com/html/html_elements.asp

w3schools.com. HTML Styles – CSS. Retrieved from
http://www.w3schools.com/html/html_css.asp

w3schools.com. HTML Color Names. Retrieved from
http://www.w3schools.com/html/html_colornames.asp

Wikipedia. HTML Attribute. Retrieved from http://en.wikipedia.org/wiki/HTML_attribute

Wikipedia (2015). Computer Security. Retrieved from
http://en.wikipedia.org/wiki/Computer_security

Wikipedia (2015). Firewall (computing). Retrieved from
http://en.wikipedia.org/wiki/Firewall_%28computing%29

Wikipedia. HTML Element. Retrieved from http://en.wikipedia.org/wiki/HTML_element

WYSIWYG Web Builder 10. Publishing your web pages. Retrieved from
http://www.wysiwygwebbuilder.com/publish.html

Web Page Mistakes How to Maintain a Website. Retrieved from
http://www.webpagemistakes.ca/maintain-website/

w3schools.com. HTML Tables. Retrieved from
http://www.w3schools.com/html/html_tables.asp

Whatis.com (2010). Cybersecuirty. Retrieved from
http://whatis.techtarget.com/definition/cybersecurity

www.ingramcontent.com/pod-product-compliance
Lightning Source LLC
Chambersburg PA
CBHW060457060326
40689CB00020B/4555